WHACK YOUR PORCUPINE

And other drawings by B. Kliban

Workman Publishing Company, New York

LIBRARY OF CONGRESS CATALOGING IN PUBLICATION DATA
KLIBAN, B.
WHACK YOUR PORCUPINE, AND OTHER DRAWINGS.
1. AMERICAN WIT AND HUMOR, PICTORIAL.   I. TITLE.
NC1429.K58A58   741.5'973   76-52861
ISBN 0-911104-92-5

DESIGN BY PAUL HANSON

WORKMAN PUBLISHING COMPANY, INC.
1 WEST 39 STREET
NEW YORK, NEW YORK 10018

MANUFACTURED IN THE UNITED STATES OF AMERICA

FIRST PRINTING APRIL 1977

20 19 18 17 16 15 14 13

This book is dedicated to:

A., B., C., D., E., F., G., H., I., J., K., L., M., N., O., P., R., S., T., U., V., W., & Z.

 – GLORIA HAS A VISIBLE ORGANISM

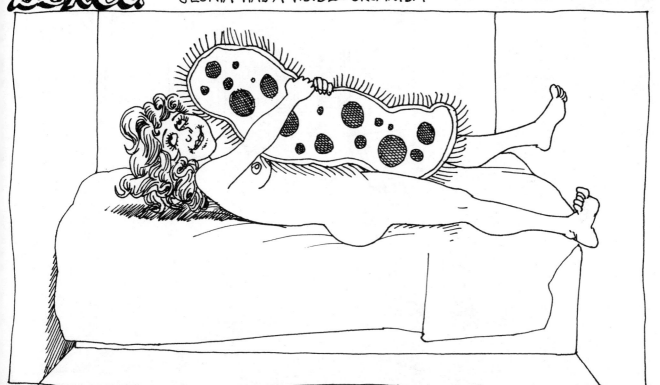

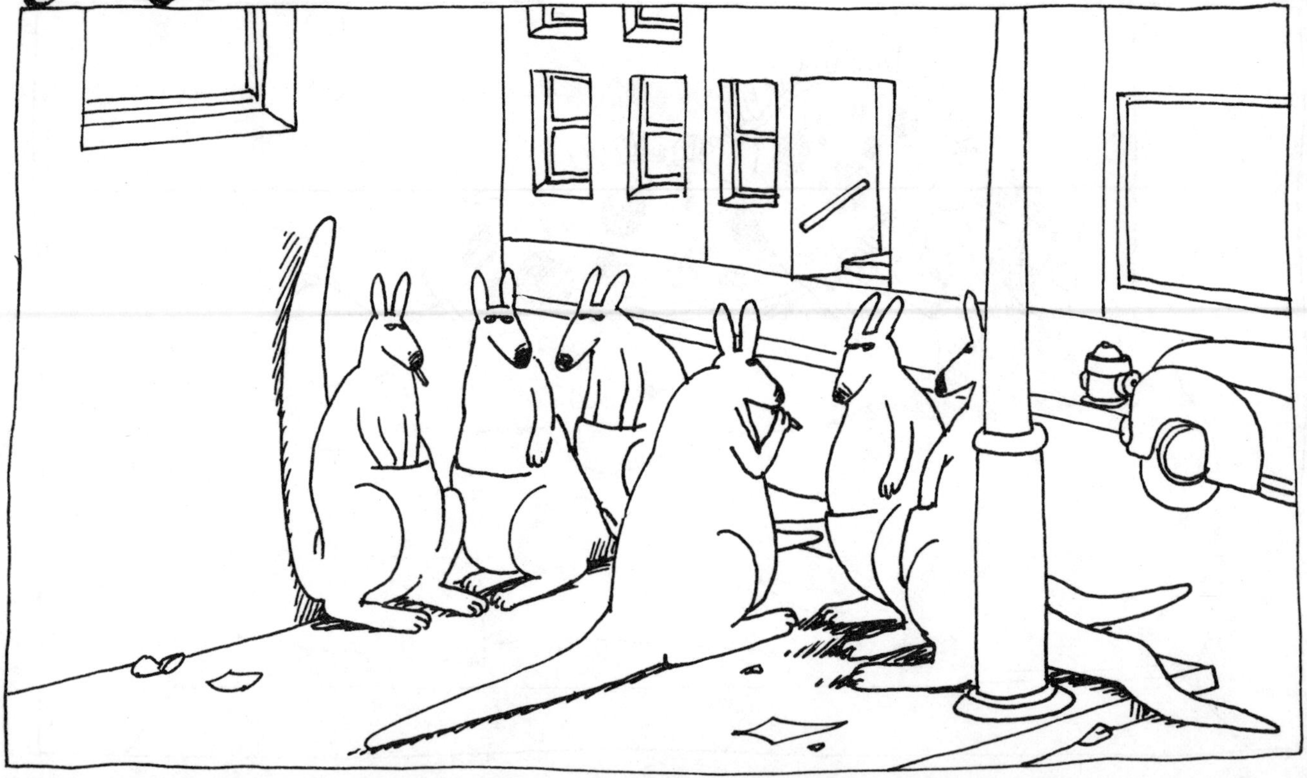

Gangaroos

That Old Devil Time

Chewing Guam

MONROE IS VISITED BY THE ORAL HYGIENE FAIRY

Destiny

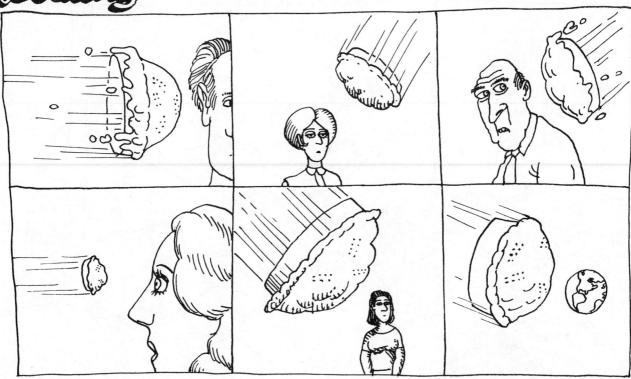

Jewish Humor

Copping A Feel

Chapter V

THE PROFESSOR AND EDGAR
VISIT NANCY,
UNBEKNOWNST TO TED.

WASTED & USEFUL LIVES

Fig.1

Fig.2

Chapter XIX

EDGAR'S INDUSTRIOUSNESS WON HIM MANY ADMIRERS.

Industrialist

Eats

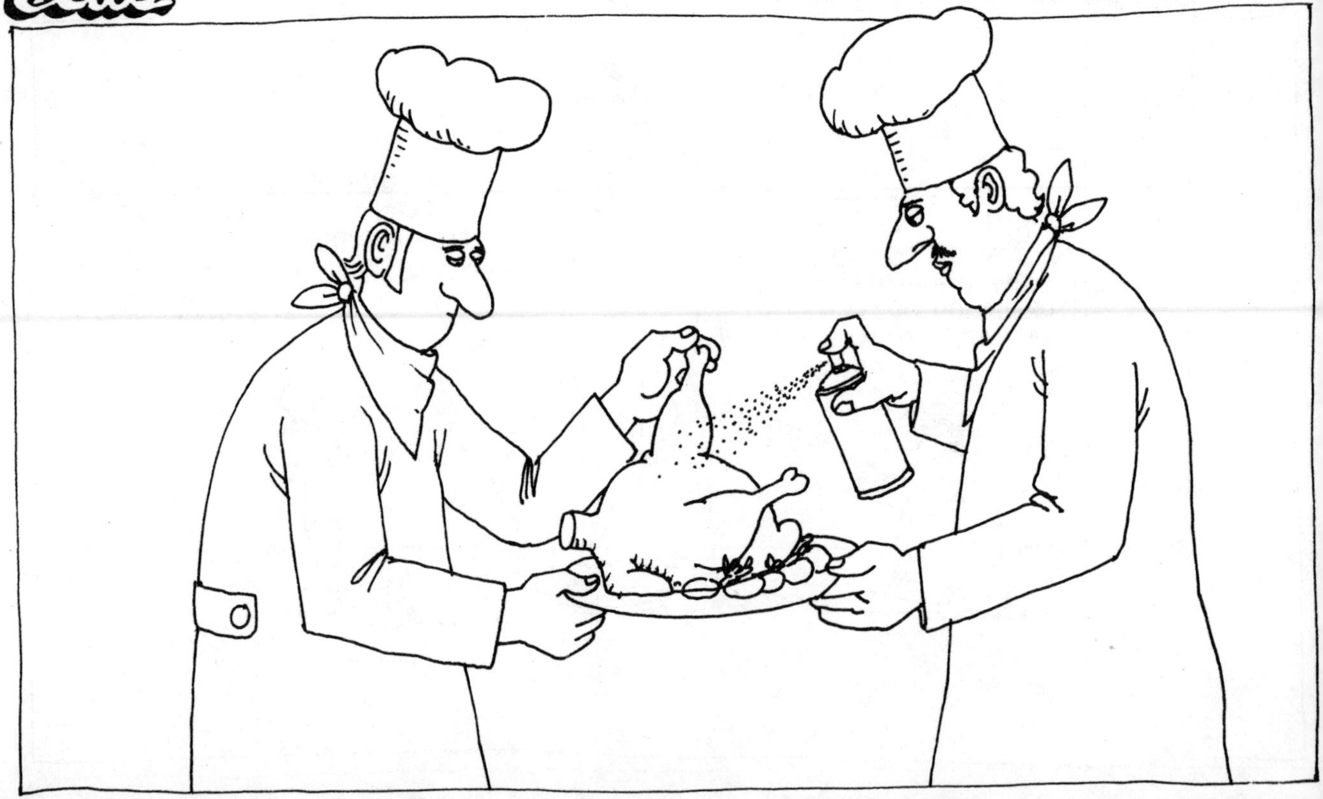

Yam Facts

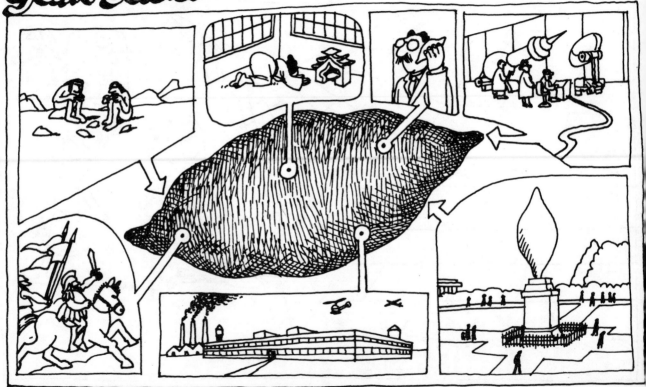

Chapter II

CARL GETS HIS PIE
IN SPITE OF FLORENCE.

ILLEGAL ALIENS FROM OUTER SPACE

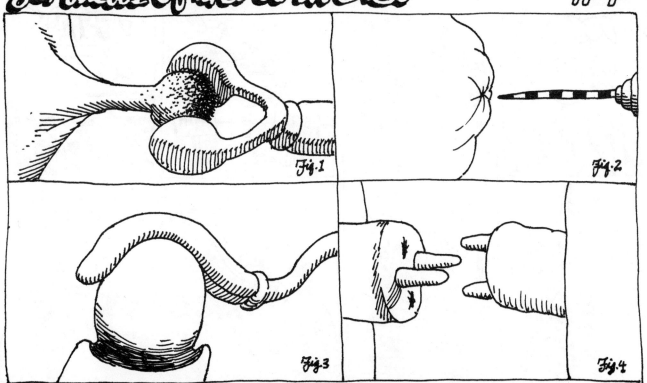

Genitals of the Universe

Fig. 1

Fig. 2

Fig. 3

Fig. 4

PIGGLY

wiggly

BIRD BATH

PIE

Cat hips

FISH LIPS.

POKE YOU IN THE EYE!

Tit Watt

THE BOREDOM OF ST. CECIL BY THE TURKS

Bus Station Pest

Our Friend Electricity

OHMS

WHATS

GROUND

POWER POLE

Astronomy

HALLEY'S COMET

HALLEY'S BREAKFAST

Grouse Pincing on the Moor

Ninnies & Cretins

Practicing Physicians

One man's mate is another man's person.

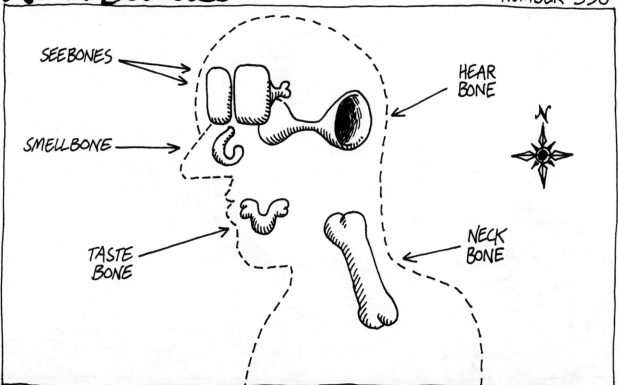

Pine Tree Point

god

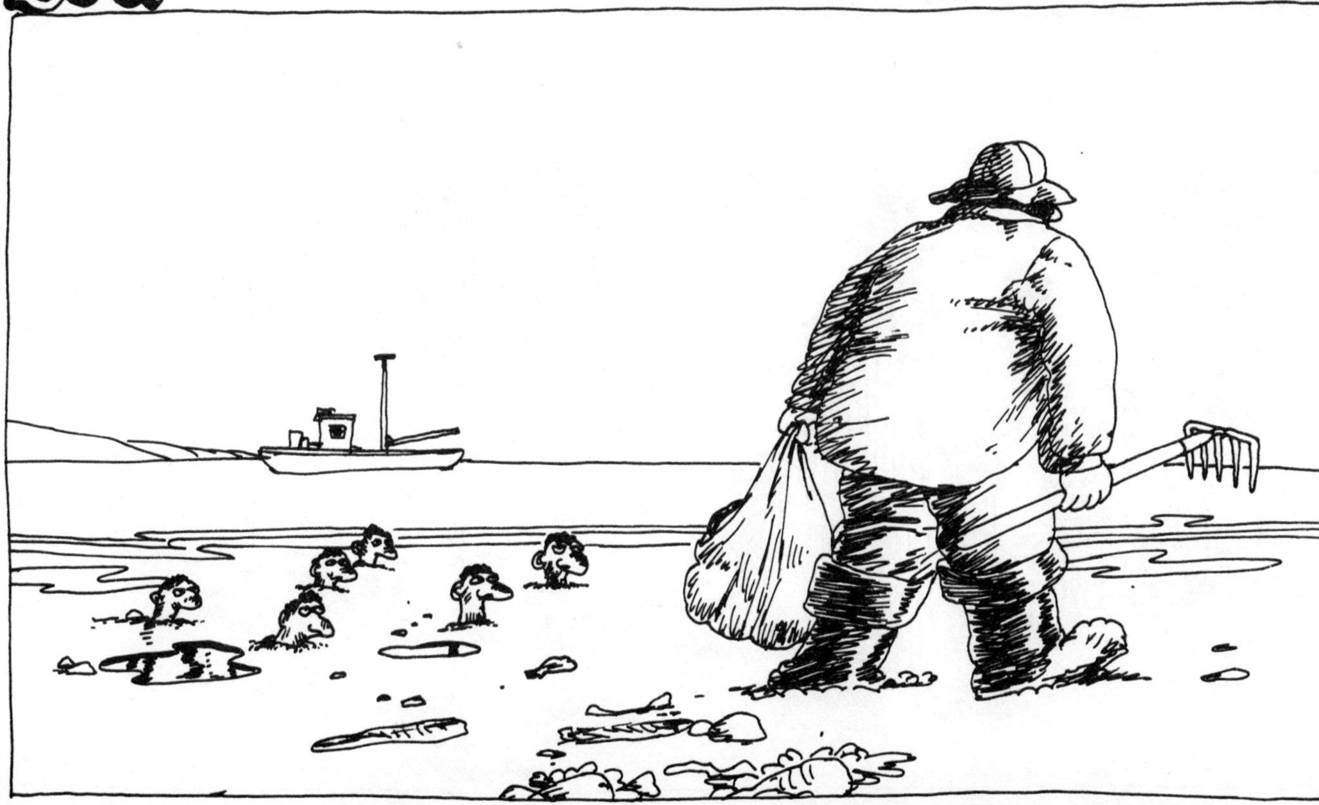

Motoring Gloves

Fig. 1

CENTRAL ASIA - TREE DWELLERS

NEVER GIVE A GUN TO DUCKS #5

History.

CLEOPATRA COMMITED SUICIDE BY HOLDING A BEAST TO HER ASS.

Fig. 1

Postures of the World #134

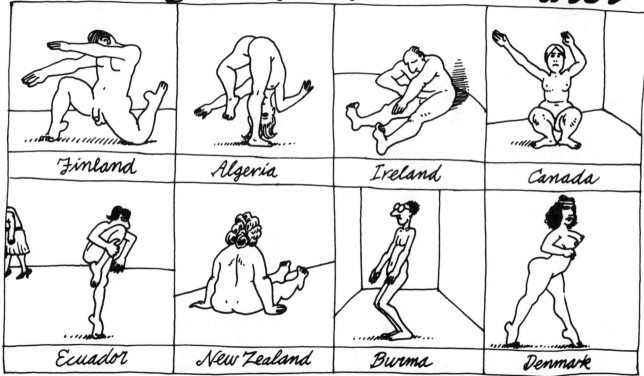

Finland

Algeria

Ireland

Canada

Ecuador

New Zealand

Burma

Denmark

Genitals of the Universe #8

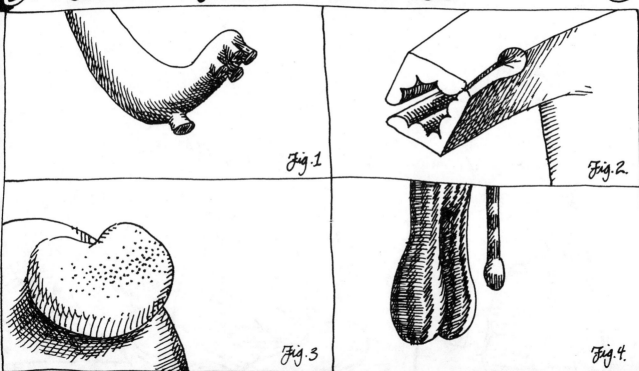

Fig.1

Fig.2

Fig.3

Fig.4

Buddha Maintenance

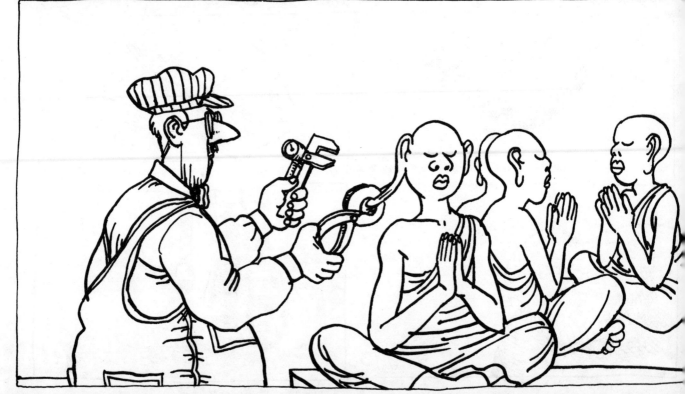

The Big Part Club

Ted Really Liked His Storks

Unhappy Bruce

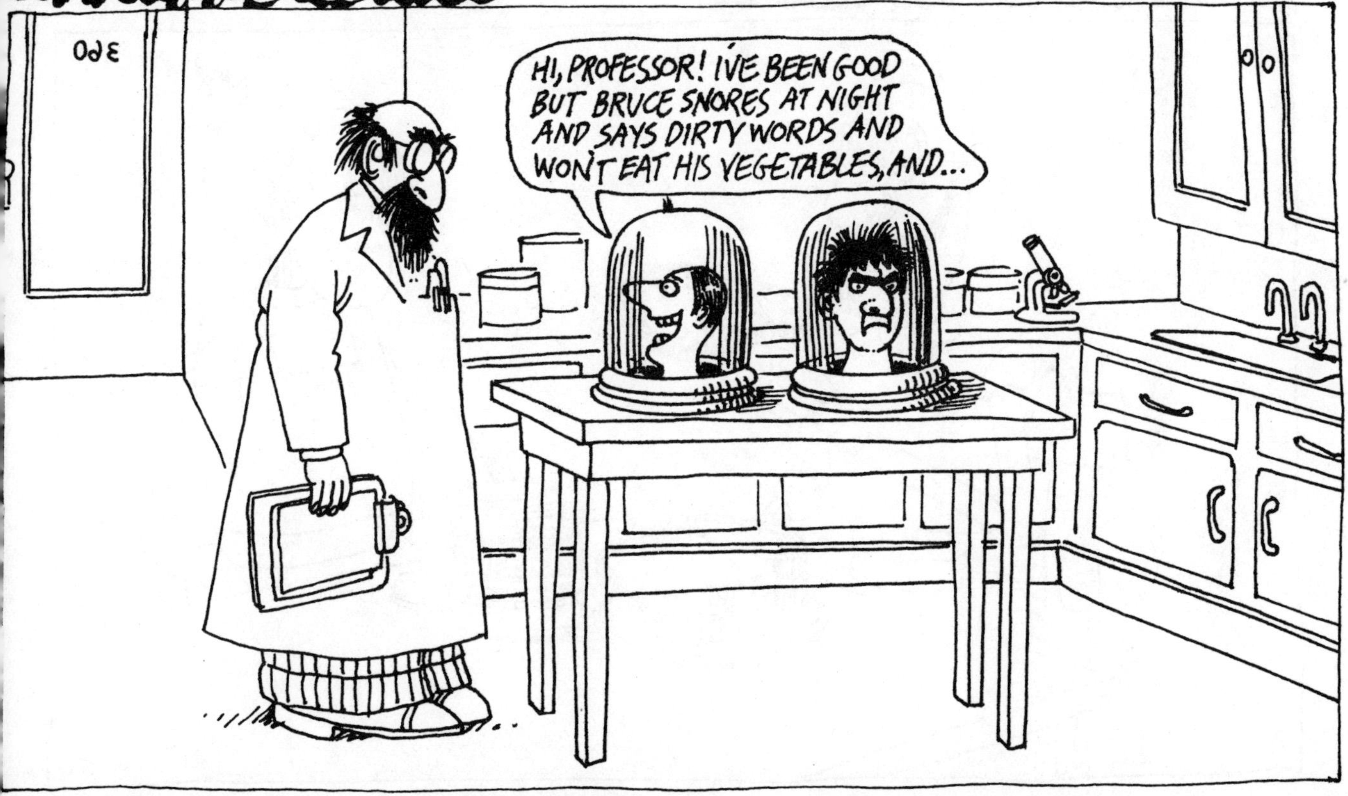

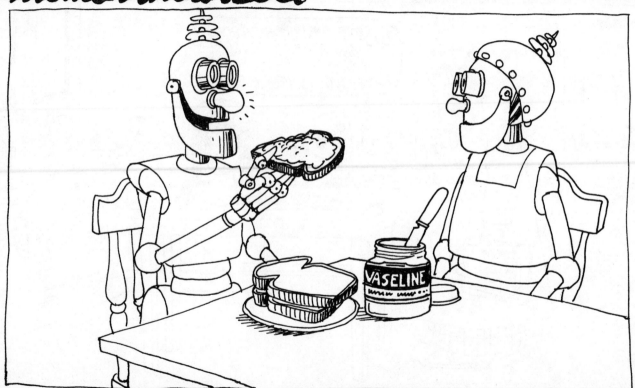

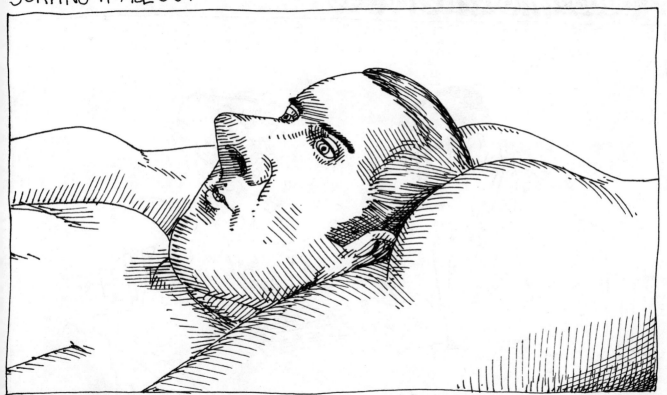

Whack Your Porcupine

Vegetables

THE VEGETABLE IN GENERAL,
DOES LITTLE TO ADMIRE.
IT OFTEN ENTERS POLITICS,
BUT SELDOM RISES HIGHER.

Miracles. THE VIRGIN MARY APPEARS TO A FOREIGN CAR IN DENVER #3

Hi!

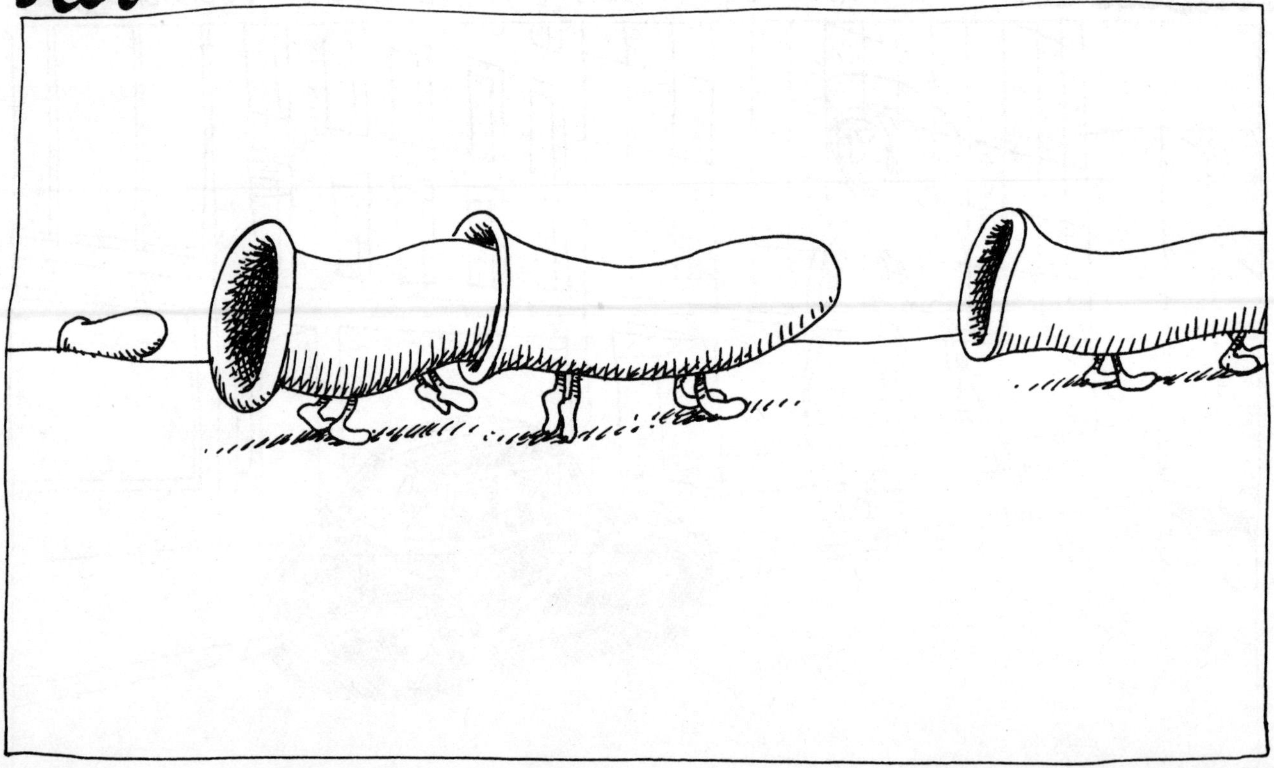

Know Your Bod

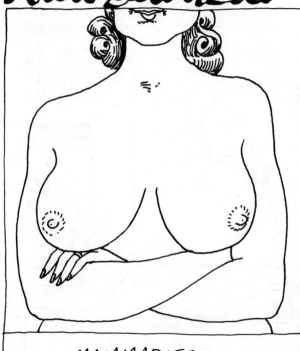

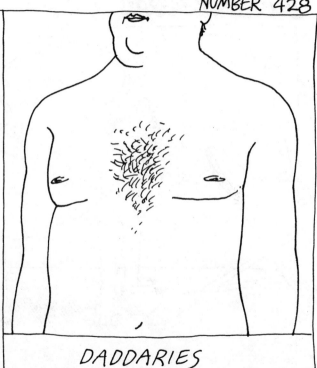

MAMMARIES

DADDARIES

Intellectual

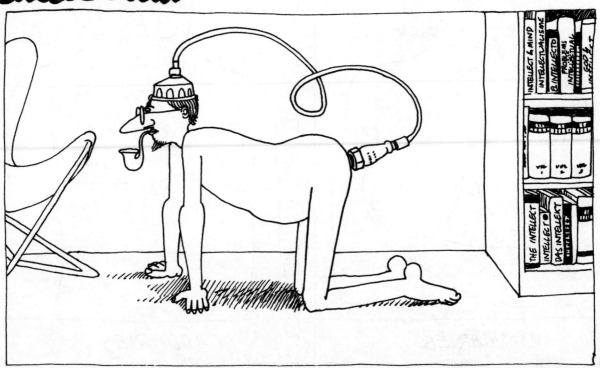

GOD MADE MONROE SIMMONS WEAR A LIME POPSICLE
AROUND HIS NECK FOR MOST OF HIS ADULT LIFE.

Pantry Hose

Data

great Moments in Medicine. #12

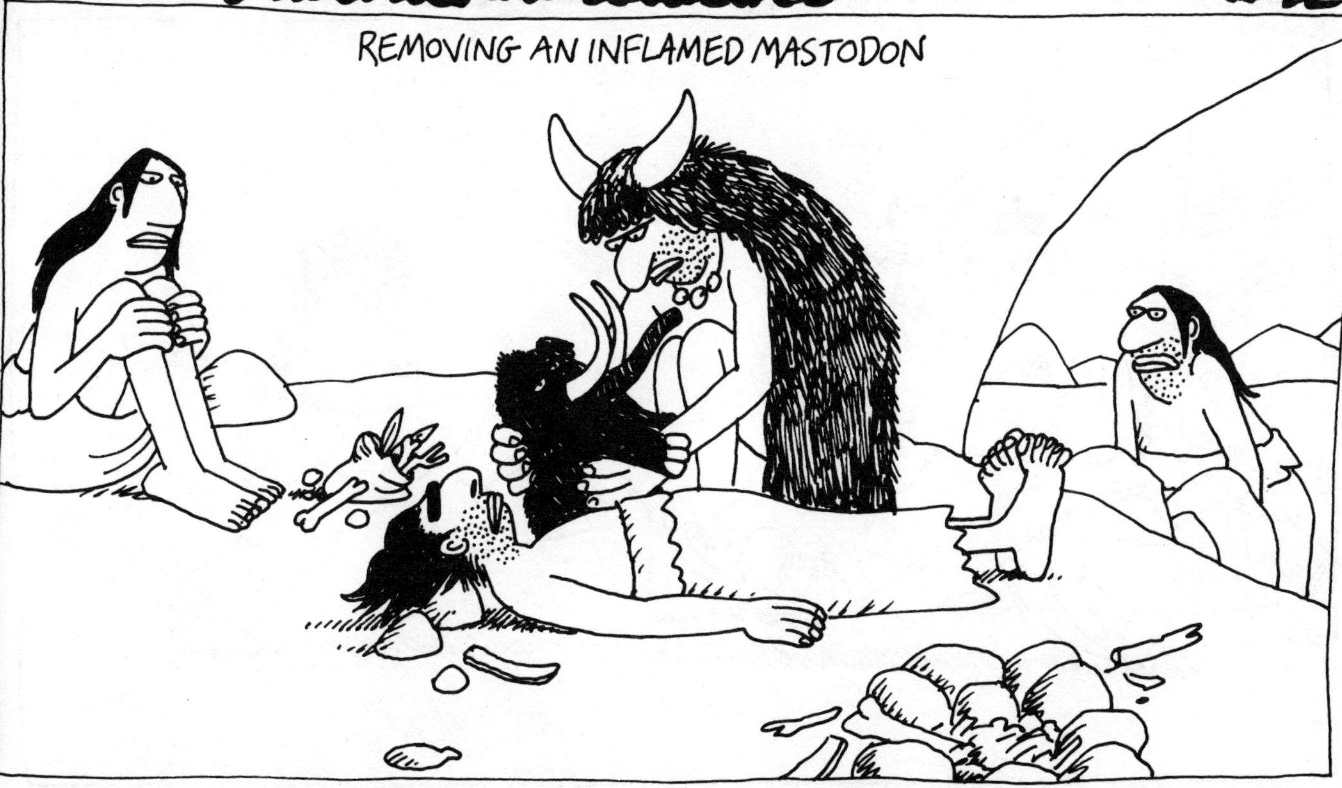

Cyril is pursued by savages

ROGER FINISHES HIS FIRST WAX FOOT

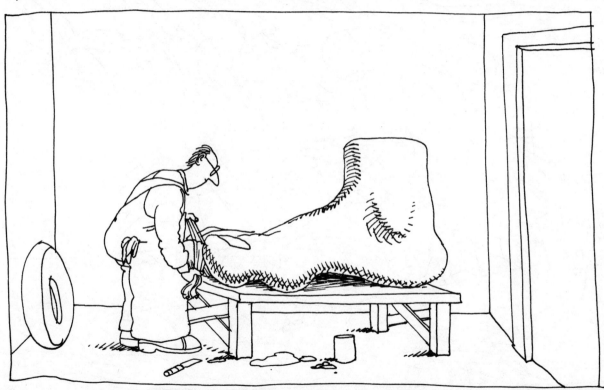

MARCH 6 75

Another Boy For Jesus

Things We Never Suspect #588

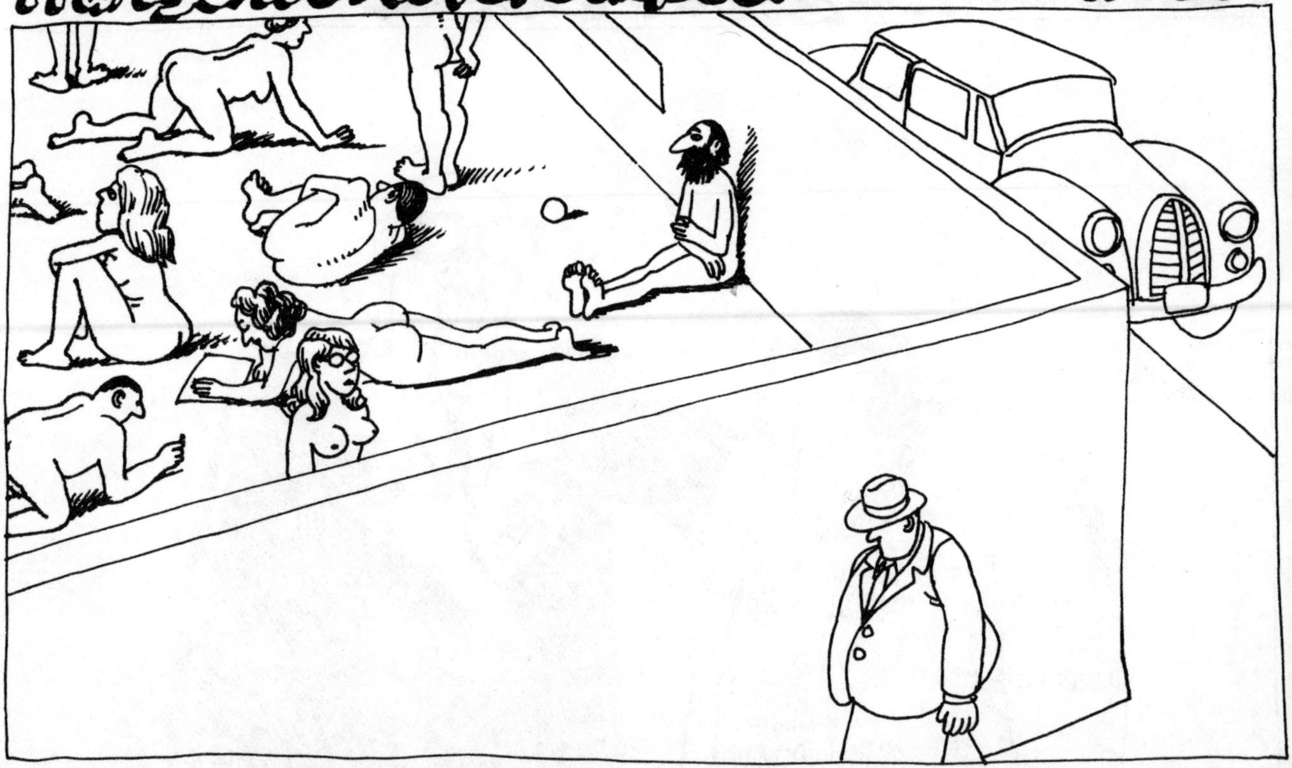

FIRST CONTACT WITH THE BEAN TRIBE

No Loitering

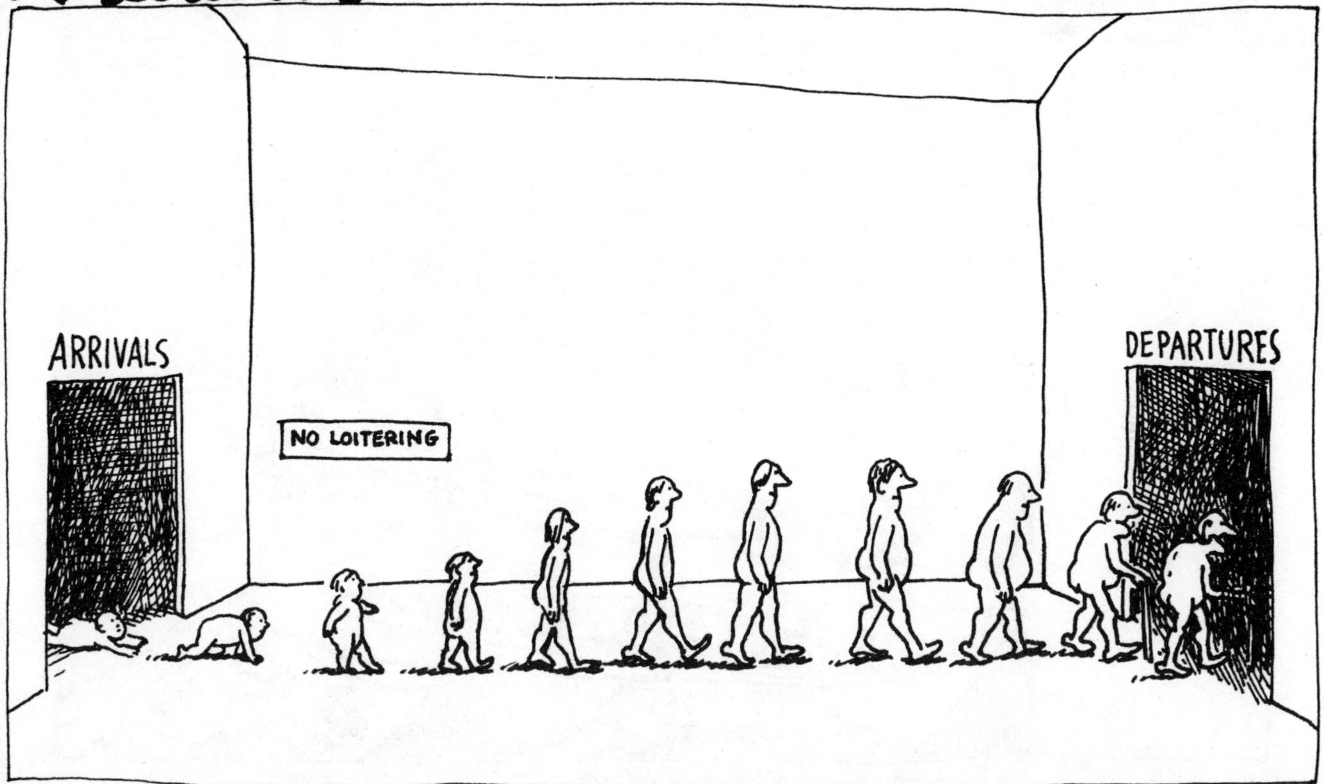

The Turk

For some reason, the following drawings emerged of their own free will over a two week period, and then stopped, for some other reason.

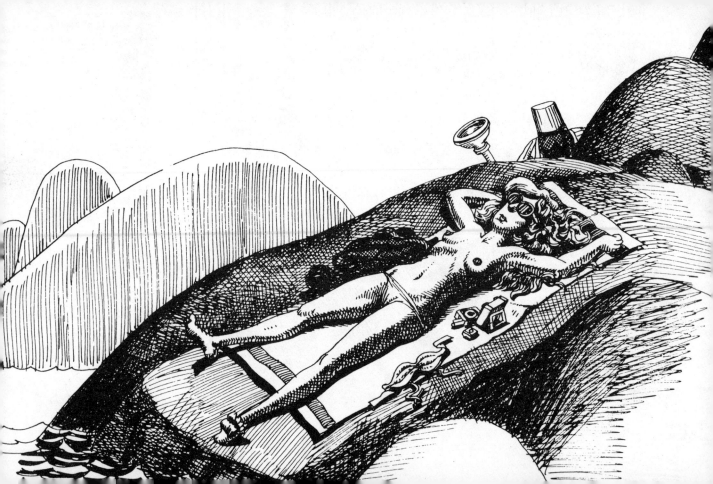

The End

Sheer Pottery

Santa Claus as a Young Man

The Lewd Sisters Soon Had Carl Aroused

The Sensory Apparatus

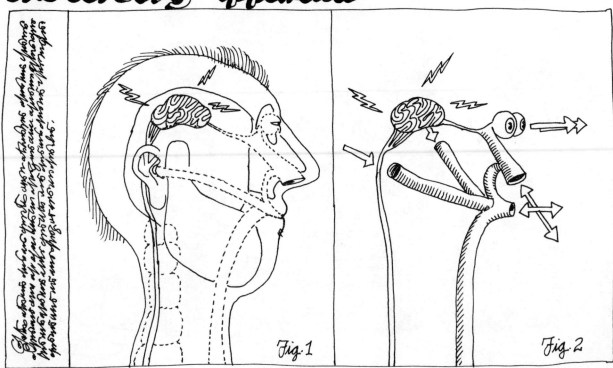

Fig. 1

Fig. 2

Chapter III

Dumb Fountain with Goose

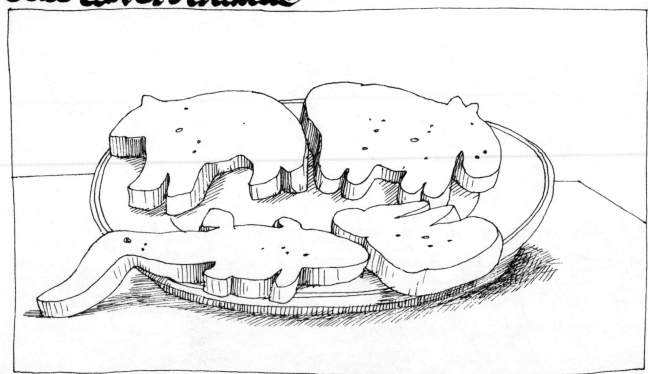

GONDOLIER ATTACKED BY RABBIS

Learning Filth in the Streets

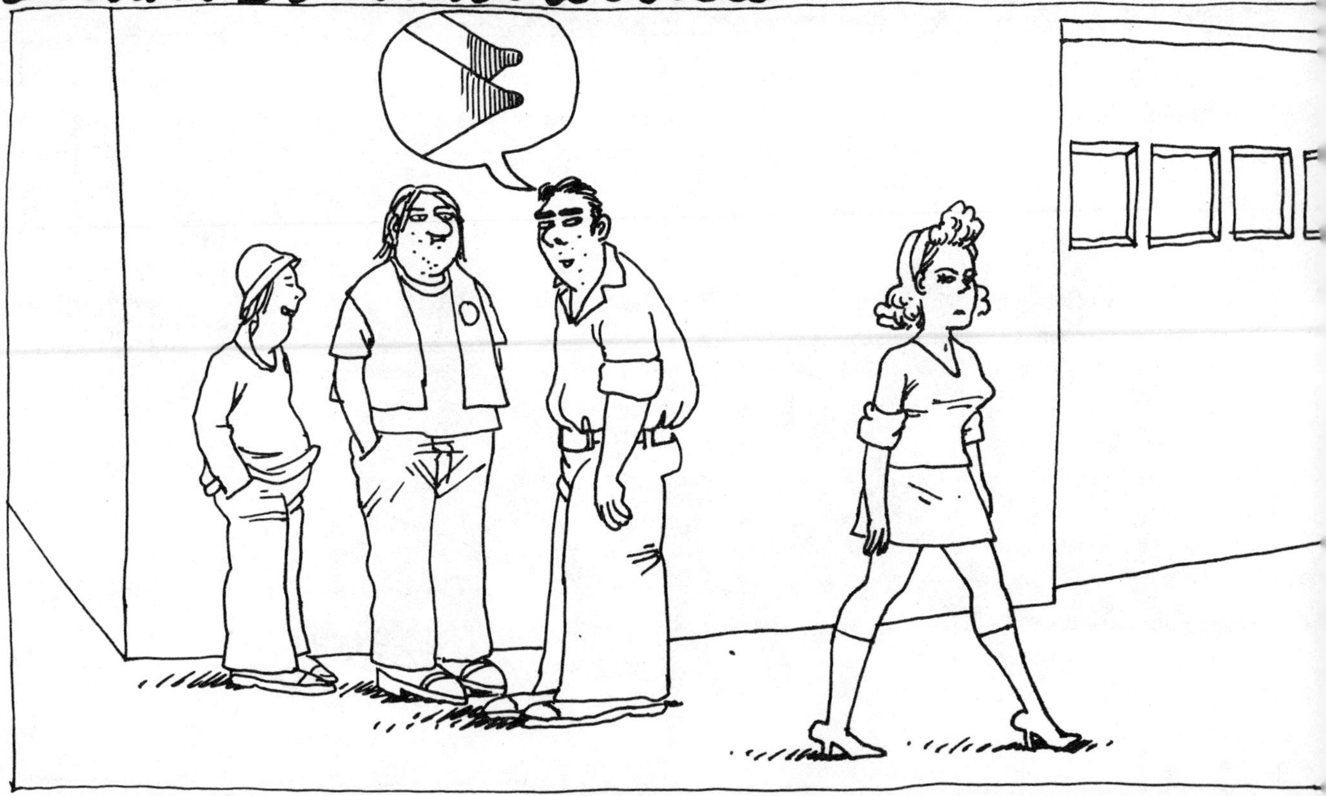

Beanism Explained

BASIC BEANBODIES

Fig. 1

Wear It Anywhere

FORMAL

CASUAL

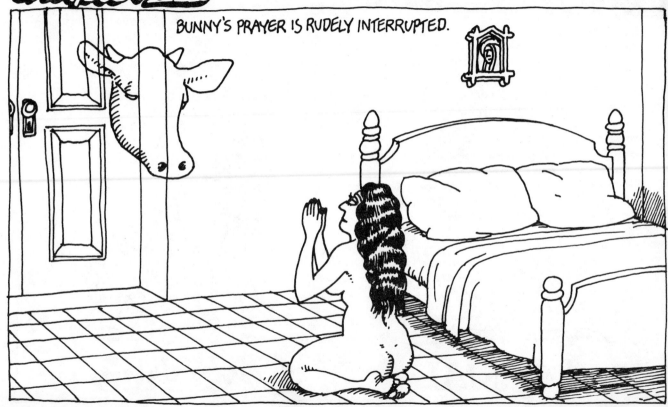

Sandy

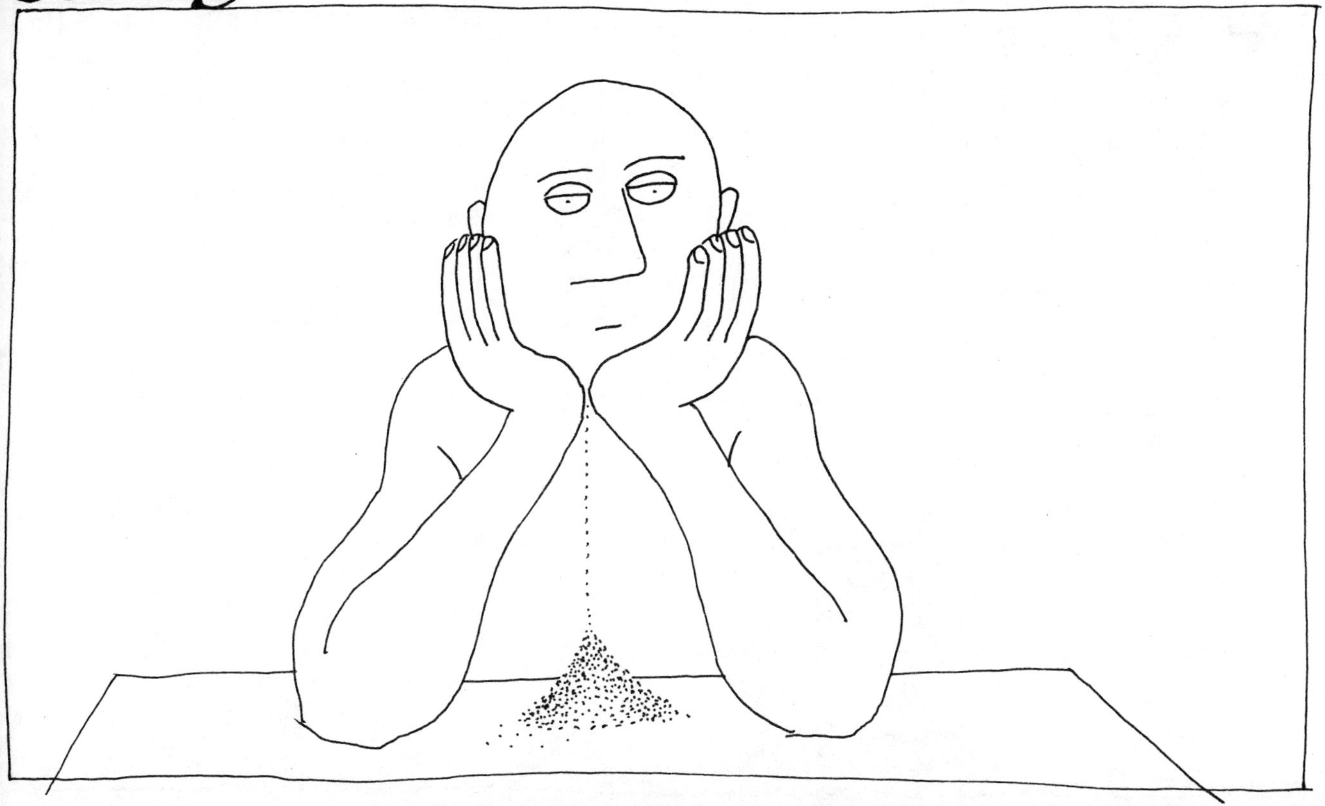

MANY PEOPLE ARE INJURED EACH YEAR BY FALLING SHEEP.

Dummies & Feebs

TED, A HANDSOME PERSON, HAD LITTLE TROUBLE WITH THE PENCILS.

ON THE STEPS OF CENTRAL ASIA WITH FLORENCE AND LEONARD.

Religions #9

MONK BANK

MONK RINK

MONK PRANK

MONK JUNK

CRAZY PEOPLE AMUSING THEMSELVES

A TERM FOR THE WURST

AARDVARK

PERCO-
LATOR

Five Cent Cigar

RHINESTONES

SOUP
BONES

MIDGETS
IN A
JAR

A.&E.

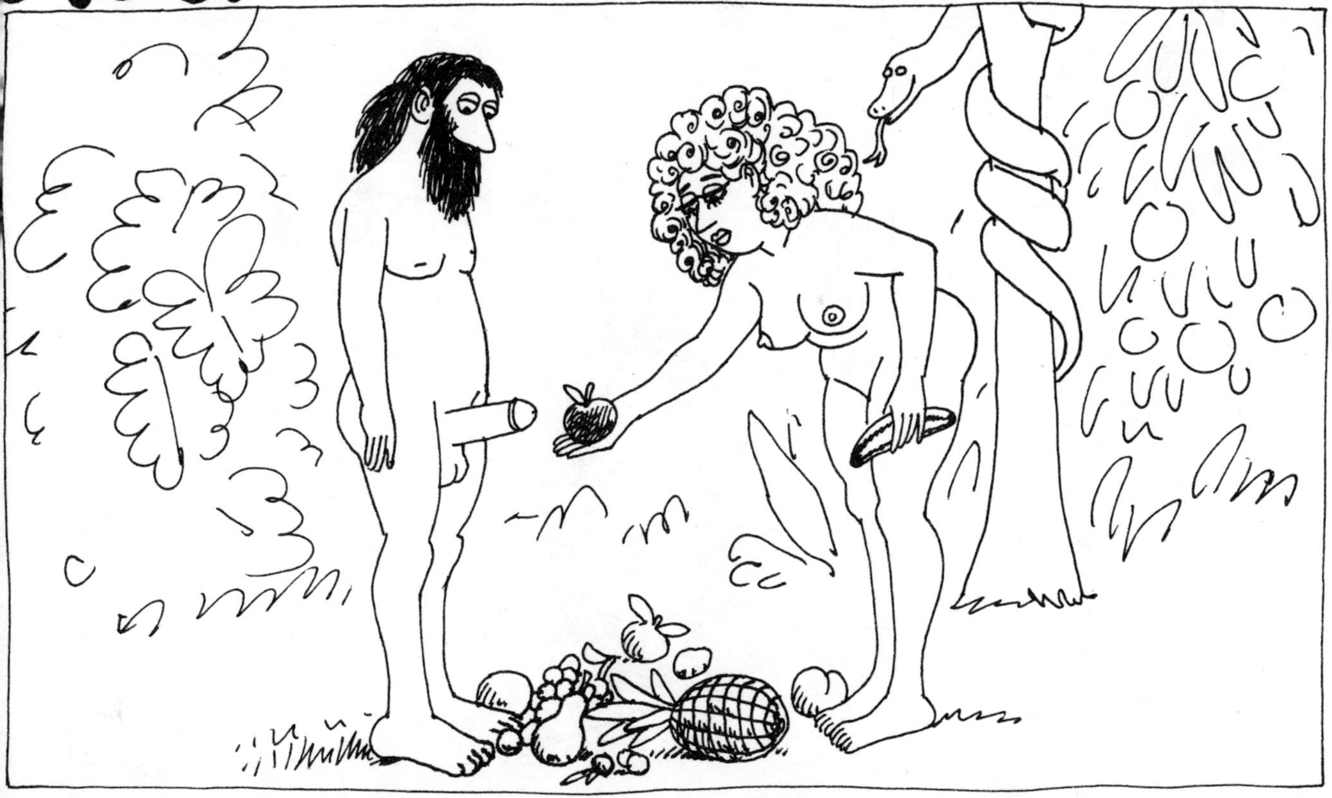

Infuriating Rubber Pan

CHEESE MAKING IN BULGARIA #17

Easy Home Test

☐ PORNOGRAPHY
☐ SMUT
☐ EROTIC ART
☐ TRASH
☐ OTHER
☐ FILTH

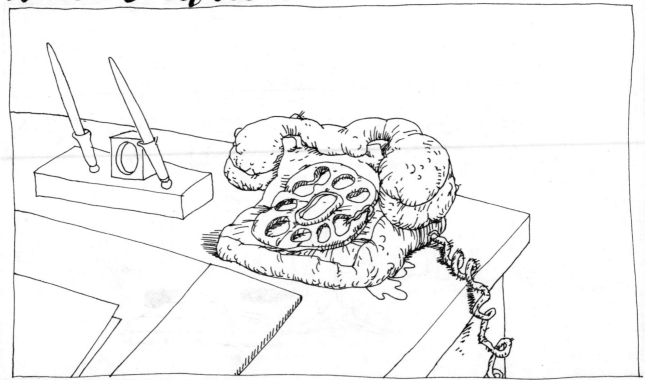

Brethren & Cistern

... BY THE TIME I GOT HOME, GRANDMOTHER HAD EATEN MOST OF THE PORCUPINES.

End

THESE CARTOONS ARENT FUNNY! YOU SHOULD BE ASHAMED OF YOURSELF!